NO HANDS ALLOWED
A Robbie Reader

David Beckham

Soccer Megastar

by Rebecca Thatcher Murcia

Mitchell Lane
PUBLISHERS

P.O. Box 196
Hockessin, Delaware 19707
Visit us on the web: www.mitchelllane.com
Comments? email us:
mitchelllane@mitchelllane.com

Printing   2   3   4   5   6   7   8   9

A Robbie Reader/No Hands Allowed

David Beckham   Landon Donovan   Josh Wolff
Freddy Adu   DaMarcus Beasley   Brian McBride
Brandi Chastain

Library of Congress Cataloging-in-Publication Data
Murcia, Rebecca Thatcher, 1962-
    David Beckham / by Rebecca Thatcher Murcia.
        p. cm.–(A Robbie reader. No hands allowed)
    Includes bibliographical references and index.
    ISBN 1-58415-384-9 (library bound)
    1. Beckham, David, 1975–Juvenile literature. 2. Soccer players–England–Biography–
Juvenile literature. I. Title. II. Series.
    GV942.7.B432M87 2005
    796.334'092–dc22
                                                                        2004024611
ISBN 13: 978-1-58415-384-9   ISBN 10: 1-58415-384-9

ABOUT THE AUTHOR: Rebecca Thatcher Murcia grew up in Garrison, New York, and graduated from the University of Massachussetts at Amherst. She was a daily newspaper reporter–mostly in Texas–for 14 years. She is a soccer coach and a player in Akron, Pennsylvania, where she lives with her husband and two sons. She is the author of another soccer biography for Mitchell Lane Publishers, *Landon Donovan* and *Freddy Adu.*
PHOTO CREDITS: cover: Denis Doyle/AFP/Getty Images; p. 3, 4: Pedro Armestre/AFP/Getty Images; p. 6: Gerry Penny/AFP/Getty Images; p. 7: Corbis; p. 8 Javier Soriano/AFP/Getty Images; p. 12 Alex Livesey/AFP/Getty Images; p. 14: top and bottom: Ross Kinnaird/AFP/Getty Images; p. 16: John Peters/AFP/Getty Images; p. 17: Shaun Botterill/AFP/Getty Images; p. 18: Phil Cole/AFP/Getty Images; p. 20: top: Gary M. Prior/AFP/Getty Images, bottom: Vincenzo Pinto/AFP/Getty Images; p. 22: AFP/Getty Images; p. 23: Alan Davidson/Wireimage; p. 24: Corbis; p. 26: Stuart Franklin/AFP/Getty Images; p. 28: Dave Hogan/AFP/Getty Images; p. 29 James Quinton/Wireimage
ACKNOWLEDGMENTS: The following story has been thoroughly researched, and to the best of our knowledge, represents a true story. While every possible effort has been made to ensure accuracy, the publisher will not assume liability for damages caused by inaccuracies in the data, and makes no warranty on the accuracy of the information contained herein. This story has not been authorized or endorsed by David Beckham or anyone associated with David Beckham.

TABLE OF CONTENTS

David Beckham, shown at the release of his new DVD, "Really Bend it Like Beckham," has become an international celebrity due to his soccer skills, his handsome face, and his sense of style.

GOOOOOOOAL!

David Beckham had just turned 23 years old and he was on the world stage. As a player for the English soccer team, Beckham was competing in the 1998 **World Cup** in France. England had to play its third match of the **tournament** against Colombia, a strong team. The game was in a stadium in Lens, in the north of France. There were more than 38,000 fans in the stadium, and millions more were watching the game on television.

About 30 minutes into the game, England was winning 1-0. The team was given a **free kick** about 30 yards away from Colombia's goal.

David Beckham celebrates his goal against Colombia at the 1998 Soccer World Cup in Lens, France.

Four members of Colombia's team formed a wall between the ball and the goal. Colombia's tall goalkeeper was crouched, ready to grab any ball that passed the wall. Most of the other Colombian players were over to one side, expecting Beckham to pass the ball.

Beckham backed away from the ball. He took a short run and kicked. The ball curled up over the wall of players. It bent into the upper left corner of the goal. The Colombian goalkeeper made a big dive toward the ball, but he fell to the ground with empty hands. Beckham had scored his first World Cup goal!

England went on to win the game 2-0. It was one of Beckham's many amazing moments on the soccer field.

Beckham is famous for his career as a soccer player. He is also well known for his looks, his fashion sense, and his marriage (MARE-ij) to singer Victoria "Posh Spice" Adams. But he is most famous for bending **corner kicks** and free kicks. He kicks the ball very hard and seems to be able to put it exactly where he wants it.

Beckham now plays for one of the best soccer teams in the world, Real (RAY-al) Madrid in Spain. He is very, very rich. But it has not been easy. He has worked hard to become the star he is.

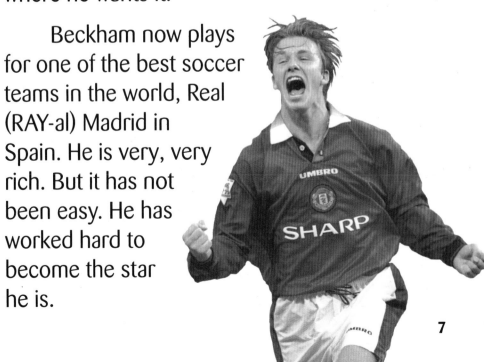

7

David Beckham is famous for his curving free kicks. In this recent photo, he shows he can also handle the sometimes tough, physical play of high-level soccer.

A SOCCER CHILDHOOD

David Robert Joseph Beckham was born in Leytonstone, an area in London, England, on May 2, 1975. His father, Ted, was a **heating engineer**. His mother, Sandra, was a hair stylist. He has two sisters, Joanne and Lynne.

Ted Beckham loved soccer and taught his son how to play from an early age. They played at a park near the Beckhams' house. Ted Beckham showed David how to kick the ball with either foot. He spent hours teaching his son many soccer skills. David also played soccer with neighborhood boys.

When David was seven, he started playing with the Ridgeway Rovers. The Ridgeway Rovers were an under-10 team. They practiced hard and went to Holland and Germany for tournaments.

Manchester United was the Beckham family's favorite team. Like the New York Yankees in American baseball, Manchester United was one of the best football teams in England and Europe. (In countries other than the United States, soccer is called football.)

David was 10 years old and becoming more serious about soccer every day. He decided to go to a sleepaway soccer camp run

David played soccer for many years to be the great soccer player that he is today.

by Bobby Charlton, one of the best English soccer players ever. But his family could not afford the $230 fee. His grandfather, also a soccer fan, paid for the camp. The first year he went there, David was not happy. He was lonely and a little homesick. But the second year at camp, he was a star.

At the age of 11, he won the camp skills competition. The prize was a trip to Barcelona, (Bar-seh-LOW-nuh) Spain, to train with Barcelona's professional (pro-FEH-shuh-nul) soccer team.

David also trained with the Tottenham Spurs, a professional team near his home. He was 13 when he had to decide: Should he sign a contract with the Tottenham Spurs, a nearby team, or with his favorite club, Manchester United? Manchester United was about 200 miles away. It would be hard for his family to take him that far.

With the support of his parents, David decided to sign with Manchester United. It was a big step—and one taken by very few 13-year-olds.

David Beckham is shown here playing for Real Madrid later in his career. He often has the speed to get to the ball first.

CHAPTER THREE

A TEENAGED STAR

David could not leave home at the age of 13. At first he trained at Old Trafford, Manchester United's home stadium, during school vacations. He played for his high school team and for a regional team.

When David was 15, he moved to Manchester to become a full-time professional soccer player. He stayed with a family that lived near the stadium. His parents came to visit him almost every weekend. Ted Beckham wanted to make sure that David did not get too proud. "You may have signed with Manchester United,

It's taken many years of practice for David to be a great soccer player. Here he is warming up before a game.

but you haven't done anything yet," he told his son.

But Beckham did start proving himself. He and other young stars formed the Manchester United youth team. They won their first tournament, the Milk Cup in Northern Ireland.

In 1992 the Manchester United youth team won the national youth championship. Beckham scored with his left foot in one of the final games. He was young—only 17—but he still wondered when he would play for Manchester United's first team.

Finally, he got his chance. Beckham played for about 20 minutes in a Manchester United game against Brighton. After that, Beckham went back to the **reserve team** for about two years.

It may have seemed like a long time for a talented young man, but Beckham was still small for his age. Manchester United had plenty of older, tougher players. Beckham was reading the Manchester newspaper in early December of 1994. He was shocked to see that the

Beckham is a fan of hip-hop music and sometimes enjoys hip-hop fashions, as well.

manager of Manchester United, Sir Alex Ferguson, planned to let some of the younger men play against Galatasaray. (ga-LAT-sar-eye), one of the best teams in Turkey. Beckham was one of the chosen players. About 30 minutes into the game, the ball rolled to Beckham near Galatasaray's goal. He kicked and scored! His first goal for Manchester United!

Beckham was in for another shock. He would be loaned to Preston North End, a lower level team, for a month. He was afraid he would lose his place at Manchester United. Still, he played hard for Preston North End. These games were good training for him. When the month was over, Manchester United needed him back. His life as a soccer star was about to begin.

Beckham celebrates a goal for Manchester United along with Juan Sebastian Veron, a Manchester United player from Argentina.

FAME CAN BE TOUGH

In 1996, at the age of 21, Beckham became a regular member of the Manchester United first team. He and the team began doing very well. In the first game of the season, Beckham did something that is very rare in soccer. He received the ball in the middle of the field, and then shot on the goal. This is something that is just not done in soccer. Nobody shoots on the goal from the middle of a full-sized soccer field. The distance—more than 50 yards, or the length of four school buses—is too far for most players. But Beckham did it. The ball soared high into the

David Beckham and Alex Ferguson, the manager of Manchester United, enjoyed a good relationship until Beckham became very famous.

Even professional soccer stars make mistakes on the field.

air, went over the goalkeeper's head, and then dropped into the goal.

A few weeks later, Beckham was watching television with his parents. The news came on with a list of English players chosen to play a game against Italy. Beckham had always dreamed of playing for his country. He could not believe his ears when he heard his name. He jumped off the sofa and hugged his mother. Over the next two years, he played in all eight games to help England qualify for the World Cup tournament. At the tournament in France in 1998, England advanced to play Argentina (Are-jen-TEEN-uh). At that stage, the team that loses is eliminated from the tournament.

England and Argentina are **arch enemies** in soccer. The match was very important. During the game, one of the players for Argentina, Diego Simeone (see-may-OH-nee), knocked Beckham down. For a moment, he lay on his stomach in frustration. Then he kicked his right foot at Simeone and knocked him down. The **referee** knew that Beckham had been fouled, but he could not forgive him for

21

David was given a red card for knocking down Diego Simeone (left) during the 1998 Soccer World Cup second round match with Argentina.

kicking Simeone. He showed Beckham the **red card** and sent him out of the game. England tied the game, 2-2, but lost on **penalty kicks**, 4-3.

English newspapers and soccer fans were mad. They blamed the loss on Beckham. There were many angry headlines, such as: TEN HEROIC LIONS AND ONE STUPID BOY.

Beckham's heart was broken. He said he was sorry. He cried. There was one thing that helped him keep going. His girlfriend, the pop singer Victoria Adams from the group Spice

Girls, had just told him that she was going to have a baby. Beckham had always wanted to be a father. His first son, Brooklyn, was born on March 4, 1999. David and Victoria had a huge wedding at a castle (KAS-il) in Ireland. They bought a large house near London.

After the 1998 World Cup, Beckham and Manchester United made English soccer history. For the first time, the team won all three major championships in the 1998–1999 season. Beckham's two corner kicks led to the two goals that won Manchester United the European championship. Beckham had once again earned the respect of reporters and soccer fans.

David with his son, Brooklyn in 2002.

David Beckham is famous for changing his haircut as often as some people change their clothes. He has worn a Mohawk, cornrows, braids, and a very short "buzz" type of cut. Some soccer writers think Beckham plays best when his hair is short.

THE WAY TO SPAIN

By 2002, Beckham was a major international (in-ter-NAH-shuh-nul) soccer star. He was also more than that. People admired his clothes. They liked his many different haircuts. Newspapers loved to print pictures of him and his beautiful wife. He was a very popular figure on and off the field. A movie about a young English girl's quest to become a soccer player, *Bend It Like Beckham,* was a big hit. Meanwhile, Romeo, a second son, was born on September 1, 2002.

Beckham was asked to captain the English team that did very well at the 2002 World Cup

In 2003, David joined Real Madrid, a Spanish soccer team that includes soccer stars from France, Brazil, and several other countries. David is in the lower right corner.

in Korea and Japan. Fans followed him around in Asia, screaming their love for him.

None of this sat well with Sir Alex Ferguson, the all-business manager of Manchester United. For many years, Ferguson had been like a second father to Beckham, but they no longer got along. Ferguson did not like the fact that Beckham and his wife lived near London, far from Manchester. He began to criticize Beckham's playing. Beckham realized he needed to find a new team.

Real Madrid, one of the few teams in the world that is more famous than Manchester United, is made up of the best players from Spain, Brazil, France, and other countries. In 2003, the team signed a four-year contract with Beckham worth up to 41 million U.S. dollars. The change did not go well at first. Real Madrid did not win any championships during Beckham's first season. Some people said he played badly and seemed lost on the Spanish soccer field.

As usual, Beckham fought on. When Real Madrid started the new season in 2004, they won their first game on a goal by Beckham. He continued to try to get used to life in Spain. By the end of 2004, he was able to speak a little more Spanish.

When the tsunami (SOO-nah-mee) disaster hit South Asia in December 2004, Beckham wanted to help the children. He became a Goodwill **Ambassador** for UNICEF, the United Nations Children's Fund. He has helped raise money for children hurt by the disaster, and he has worked to bring soccer and other sports to those children. Meanwhile, a third son, Cruz, was born on February 20, 2005.

In March 2005, Beckham started a soccer school, The David Beckham Academy, in London, near where he grew up. He plans to hold soccer camps during school vacations and offer free training days during the school year.

Beckham and his wife, Victoria, often organize events to raise money for needy children.

"To see the happiness that football (soccer) brings to kids, that is the most important thing," Beckham said. He is also planning to open a sister school at the Home Depot Center near Los Angeles, California in the summer of 2005.

Only time will tell whether Beckham can be everything he wants to be: soccer superstar, pop figure, ambassador, and family man. But if the past can help tell the future, he will once again surprise everyone.

David is shown with some young soccer fans at the launch of his new soccer school, The David Beckham Football Academy in March 2005.

1975 born on May 2 in Leytonstone, England

1991 signs a youth training scheme contract with Manchester United

1993 signs a professional contract with Manchester United

1996 is picked to play regularly for United's first team on September 1

1998 at the World Cup in France, scores first goal for England on June 26

1999 son Brooklyn Joseph Beckham is born on March 4; marries Victoria "Posh Spice" Adams on July 4; Manchester United makes history by being the first English team to win the English Football Association Cup, the Premier League championship, and the European Champions League all in the same year

2000 captains the English national team for the first time on November 15

2002 son Romeo Beckham born on September 1

2003 signs with Real Madrid in Spain; begins playing for them in July; *Beckham: Both Feet on the Ground: An Autobiography* is published

2004 scores the first goal in Real Madrid's first game in the new 2004–2005 season

2005 becomes UNICEF Goodwill Ambassador; third son, Cruz, born February 20; opens the David Beckham Football Academy in London, England

Ambassador –(am-BASS-uh-der)–an official title for a person who represents a country or an organization.

arch enemies–(arch EN-neh-mees)–main opponents or foes.

corner kick–a free kick that the attacking team gets to make from the corner of the field when a defender sends the ball over the end line near the defending team's goal.

free kick–an unopposed kick given to a team when the referee decides someone on that team was fouled. Free kicks are also awarded when an opponent touches the ball with a hand or arm.

heating engineer–a person who designs and repairs systems that keep buildings warm.

penalty kick –the goalkeeper must stay on the goal line while an opposing player kicks the ball from the penalty spot, about 12 yards away.

red card–a card that a referee shows to a player who has done something very wrong in a soccer game. The player has to leave the game and miss the next game.

referee–the person responsible for making sure both teams follow the rules of the game.

reserve team–players who are members of a professional team but have not been chosen to play in the team's major games.

tournament–(TUR-na-ment)–a series of games that leads to a championship.

World Cup–the international championship for outdoor soccer.

TO FIND OUT MORE

Magazine Articles

Marcotti, Gabriele. "The World's Most Popular Team: Manchester United Invades America This Summer." *Sports Illustrated for Kids,* July 1, 2003.
You might enjoy the photographs in:
Davy, Emma. "Trick Kick." *Current Science,* August 29, 2003, p. 4.

Web Addresses

The English National Team
www.theFA.com
David Beckham Academy
www.thedavidbeckhamacademy.com

The Real Madrid Soccer Team
www.realmadrid.com
The World Soccer Federation
www.fifa.com

Works Consulted

Beckham, David, and Tom Watts. *Beckham: Both Feet on the Ground.* New York: HarperCollins, 2003.
Morgan, Gaynor. *The Real David Beckham: An Intimate Biography.* London: Metro Publishing, 2004.

INDEX